Mastering Raspberry Pi

DIY Projects and Ideas

Table of Contents

Chapter 1. Introduction

Special Report: Mastering Raspberry Pi: DIY Projects and Ideas

Are you ready to explore the fascinating world of the Raspberry Pi? Be it assembling your very own retro gaming console, transforming your home into a smart one, or building a pocket-sized computer, the possibilities with this credit card-sized gadget are boundlessly exciting. Our comprehensive Special Report on 'Mastering Raspberry Pi: DIY Projects and Ideas' has been crafted with the sole objective of simplifying technical jargons and complexities. This report will not only fuel your imagination with a plethora of DIY project ideas but will also meticulously guide you on your journey from being a novice to a Raspberry Pi maestro. So, dive in and let your innovative spirit take flight –creating and learning about technology has never been more thrilling!

Chapter 2. Getting Started with Raspberry Pi

Before venturing into the exciting projects, it is fundamental to first set up your Raspberry Pi and understand its basics. This chapter will navigate you through, right from unboxing your Raspberry Pi to running your first program on it.

2.1. Essential Raspberry Pi Components

When you unbox your Raspberry Pi, the primary components you'll find are the circuit board itself which hosts the CPU, GPU, RAM, USB ports, Ethernet port, and slots for HDMI, SD card, and power supply.

Some models like Raspberry Pi Zero, may not include all these elements due to their slim design. However, a Standard Raspberry Pi model will include these components:

- Central Processing Unit (CPU)

- Graphics Processing Unit (GPU)

- Random Access Memory (RAM)

- USB ports

- Ethernet port

- HDMI slot

- SD card slot

- Power supply slot

You'll notice your Raspberry Pi doesn't have a hard drive. This is because the Raspberry Pi uses an SD Card as a hard drive, which is inserted into the SD Card slot.

2.2. Necessary Peripherals

Apart from these, there are also some essential peripherals you'll need to start using your Raspberry Pi. These include:

- Power Supply: A standard Micro USB power supply works well. Ensure the power supply can produce at least 3A at 5V for a Raspberry Pi 3 or 2.5A for a Raspberry Pi 4.

- SD Card: We recommend an 8GB class 4 SD card – ideally preinstalled with NOOBS.

- Display and Connectivity Cables: You'll need an HDMI cable for the display, as well as a keyboard and mouse for navigation.

- Case : Although not mandatory but highly recommended. A case can protect the Raspberry Pi from dust and damage.

2.3. Setting up the Raspberry Pi

Once you have all the necessary components and peripherals, setting up the Raspberry Pi comprises of the following main steps:

1. Insert the SD Card into the Raspberry Pi's SD Card slot.

2. Plug the USB keyboard and USB mouse into the USB ports on the Raspberry Pi.

3. Connect your Raspberry Pi to the display using the HDMI Cable.

4. Connect the Ethernet cable from your network router to Raspberry Pi for internet connectivity.

2.4. Booting up the Raspberry Pi

After successfully connecting all the peripherals, you can boot the

Raspberry Pi:

1. Plug in the power supply into the Raspberry Pi and the wall socket. The Raspberry Pi will start to boot up once the power is switched on.

2. On the screen, you should see a rainbow screen, followed by the Raspberry Pi logo and then lines of system text. Eventually, the Raspberry Pi will boot into the Raspbian desktop or terminal, depending on your pi setup.

Although Raspbian is the official Operating System for the Raspberry Pi, there are others like Ubuntu Mate, Snappy Ubuntu Core, Windows 10 IoT Core, OSMC, LibreELEC, and even Android!

2.5. Your First Program on Raspberry Pi

By now, you should have a working Raspberry Pi system with Raspbian (or the Operating System you chose) running on it. We'll be using Python as our programming language to write our first program. Python is a great choice for beginners and is extremely powerful with many packages available for doing almost anything!

1. Open the Python 3 IDLE from the Menu → Programming → Python 3 (IDLE).

2. Go to File → New File. A new window will open.

3. Write the following lines of code:

```
print('Welcome to the world of Raspberry Pi!')
```

1. Save your file with '.py' extension like 'hello.py'.

2. To run your code, click on Run → Run Module or simply press F5.

You should see the console output "Welcome to the world of Raspberry Pi!". Congratulations on running your first program on the Raspberry Pi! Practice Python and start working on projects to fully tap into the potential of Raspberry Pi.

This chapter aimed to acquaint you with your Raspberry Pi, peripheral connections, booting up process, and running your first program. Do not worry if you did not grasp everything in one go. The beauty of learning is in repetition and persistence. The more you experiment, the more experienced you will become. Move forward and explore more exciting applications of Raspberry Pi. Your journey just got started!

Chapter 3. Hardware Basics: A Closer Look at Raspberry Pi

The Raspberry Pi devices come in different models, each with its unique features, specifications, and use-cases. Over the years, these tiny computers have evolved dramatically, leading to improved computational power, added functionalities, and diversified modularity.

3.1. Introducing Raspberry Pi

First debuting in 2012 by the Raspberry Pi Foundation, an organization aimed at promoting teaching of basic computer science, Raspberry Pi has since become a revolution in its own right. At its core, it's a single-board computer, being no larger than a credit card but having functionalities akin to a full-sized desktop.

3.2. Understanding the Various Models

As per their chronological introduction and enhancements, several Raspberry Pi models resonate with technology enthusiasts globally. A quick review presents us with:

1. Raspberry Pi 1 Model B – Introduced in 2012, with 512MB RAM.

2. Raspberry Pi 1 Model A – A cheaper variant of Model B, with 256MB RAM.

3. Raspberry Pi 1 Model B+ – An upgrade over Model B, enhancing GPIO capabilities.

4. Raspberry Pi 1 Model A+ – GPIO capabilities similar to Model B+ but cheaper, with 256MB RAM.

5. Raspberry Pi 2 – Unveiled in 2015, Quad-core CPU, 1GB RAM.

6. Raspberry Pi Zero – A miniaturized version of Model B+, costing just $5.

7. Raspberry Pi 3 – Introduced in 2016, Quad-core 64-bit CPU, onboard WiFi and Bluetooth.

8. Raspberry Pi Zero W – A Zero model with added WiFi and Bluetooth.

9. Raspberry Pi 3 Model B+ – Enhanced WiFi, more GPIO, updated CPU.

10. Raspberry Pi 4 Model B – Currently the highest performing model, it introduced in 2019, boasts up to 8GB RAM, two HDMI ports, and USB 3.0.

3.3. Understanding Raspberry Pi Components

The Raspberry Pi houses several components that help it function as a fully-fledged computer. We'll examine these vital components and their functionalities in detail.

3.3.1. Processor

The Raspberry Pi 4, the most advanced model, has a Broadcom BCM2711 Quad-core Cortex-A72 (ARM v8) 64-bit SoC running at 1.5GHz. Lower models pack different processors, but the central concept remains the same: to provide computing power.

3.3.2. GPU

Raspberry Pi integrates a powerful VideoCore VI Graphics processor, capable of handling multimedia, perfect for graphic-intensive applications and gaming.

3.3.3. RAM

The Raspberry Pi 4 offers options ranging from 2GB to 8GB LPDDR4-3200 SDRAM. This memory allows applications to store data temporarily for quick access during operation.

3.3.4. GPIO

One of Raspberry Pi's highlights is its General Purpose Input/Output (GPIO) interface. It's a generic pin on a chip whose behavior, input or output, can be controlled by the user at runtime. The GPIO pins enable the Raspberry Pi to interact with the outside world and are essential in DIY projects involving sensors, motors, and other devices.

3.3.5. Storage

Raspberry Pi recommends using a MicroSD Card loaded with NOOBS for first-time users. MicroSD acts as the disk drive for the Raspberry Pi and can hold the Operating System and software applications.

3.3.6. USB Ports

The Raspberry Pi 4 Model B comes with two USB 2.0 ports and two USB 3.0 ports for peripheral connection.

3.3.7. Network Connectivity

Raspberry Pi normally includes an ethernet port for wired network connections. In addition, wireless connectivity is available via an integrated wireless LAN adapter. Bluetooth is also incorporated, allowing connection with various wireless devices.

In essence, the Raspberry Pi introduces you to an exciting blend of programming, electronics, and innovative DIY projects. By understanding the hardware, you'll be in a better position to execute your own creations and concepts. It's scarcely been easier - or more enjoyable - to learn about technology, encapsulated within a device that can easily sit in the palm of your hand. Do remember, as you experiment and learn, the only limit you'll encounter with a Raspberry Pi is your own imagination. Happy Tinkering!

Chapter 4. Understanding Raspberry Pi Operating Systems

We begin your Raspberry Pi journey with a comprehensive understanding of its operating systems. A Raspberry Pi, though powerful, is quite futile without an operating system (OS) to bridge the hardware-software interaction.

An OS works as the intermediate layer that communicates instructions from the user to the physical Raspberry Pi hardware elements. Generally, Raspberry Pi uses Linux-based operating systems, although others like RISC OS can be loaded onto the device according to your specific requirements.

First and foremost, let's learn about the most popular operating system for Raspberry Pi which is Raspbian.

4.1. Raspbian OS

Named by combining 'Raspberry Pi' and 'Debian,' Raspbian is the official, free operating system released in 2015 by the Raspberry Pi Foundation. Based on Debian, one of the oldest and most secure Linux distributions, Raspbian provides the perfect platform to use the full graphic capabilities of the Raspberry Pi.

Raspbian OS comes pre-installed with tools and applications, including Python and Scratch programming environments, LibreOffice Suite, Chromium web browser, and Minecraft Pi edition, among others. The lightweight LXDE desktop environment and X.Org display server in the OS contribute to a low resource usage, ensuring optimal performance.

Although Raspbian is the most common choice, other Raspberry Pi-compatible OSs also exist, granting flexibility in picking a choice appropriate to your project.

4.2. Ubuntu MATE for Pi

MATE is a desktop environment derived from GNOME2 and Ubuntu MATE is a flavor (variant) of Ubuntu that uses MATE, thus named Ubuntu MATE. It's a more streamlined option that works well on Raspberry Pi. This OS is lightweight, user-friendly, and comes with basic computing programs like LibreOffice, Firefox, and Thunderbird. A notable addition is the Welcome app, which makes it easier for new users to get started.

4.3. OSMC and LibreELEC: Media Center OS

Both OSMC and LibreELEC exist for a specific purpose: turn your Raspberry Pi into a dedicated media center. OSMC (Open Source Media Center) is based on Debian, but with an emphasis on a polished interface and easy set-up process. Meanwhile, LibreELEC (Libre Embedded Linux Entertainment Center) is a smaller, stripped-down OS that exclusively runs the Kodi open-source media player.

4.4. Windows 10 IoT Core

While it's not a typical desktop version, Windows 10 IoT Core allows Raspberry Pi users to integrate their device into the Windows environment. This OS is aimed at developers and business users who want to create IoT (Internet of Things) solutions.

4.5. RISC OS Pi

Although not Linux-based, this is worth mentioning. RISC OS Pi is a fast and compact OS designed in Cambridge, England, specifically for the ARM chipset. It works beautifully on Raspberry Pi and is notable for being very lightweight, able to boot from cold in under 5 seconds.

4.6. CHOOSING THE RIGHT OPERATING SYSTEM

Choosing the right OS depends on your project requirements. Each operating system offers unique characteristics that make it the best fit for certain applications or tasks. While Raspbian is the jack of all trades, the other operating systems excel in specialized applications.

Once you've decided on the OS you wish to use, the following step is to install it on your Raspberry Pi.

4.7. INSTALLING AN OPERATING SYSTEM

The Raspberry Pi Imager is the official tool for installing an operating system on your Pi. Let's take a step-by-step look at the installation process.

- Download the imager from the official Raspberry Pi website.

- Open the imager.

- Choose the OS you want to install from the list available.

- Select the memory card you will use for the installation.

- Then click on 'WRITE' – this will install the selected OS on your card.

After following these steps, you should have your Raspberry Pi booted up, and your chosen OS should appear.

To summarize, understanding the operating systems compatible with your Raspberry Pi will guide you to choose the most suitable one suited to your needs. With this understanding and the knowledge to install an OS, you are now one step closer to transforming your ideas into reality.

Chapter 5. Essential Raspberry Pi Commands

The Raspberry Pi operates with the help of Linux, a powerful open-source operating system. To unlock the full potential of your Raspberry Pi, it's imperative to gain a solid understanding of basic Linux commands.

5.1. Understanding the Linux Command Line

The Linux command line is an efficient, powerful tool. It's often more convenient to perform complex operations using the command line than using a Graphical User Interface (GUI). The command line also enables you to communicate directly with your Raspberry Pi and execute tasks with precision.

5.2. Basic Raspberry Pi Commands

1. `pwd` (Print Working Directory): Wield this command to know which directory (folder) you're currently working in. The command `pwd` will display the path of your current directory.

2. `cd` (Change Directory): This command helps in navigating through various directories. For instance, to change your current directory to the 'Documents' directory, type `cd Documents`.

3. `ls` (List): Use this command to view the content of your current directory. Upon typing `ls`, you will see all the files and subdirectories within the present directory.

4. `cat` (Concatenate): Utilize this command to view the content of a file without having to open it. For an instance, to view the content of a file named 'file1.txt', type `cat file1.txt`.

5. `nano` : This command opens a terminal-based text editor named Nano. If you want to edit a file named 'file1.txt', type `nano file1.txt`.

6. `reboot` : It allows you to restart your Raspberry Pi from the command line.

7. `shutdown` : This Raspberry Pi command will safely power down your Pi.

5.3. File and Directory Commands

1. `cp` (Copy): Copy files or directories with `cp`. For instance, to copy a file named 'file1.txt' to another file named 'file2.txt', type `cp file1.txt file2.txt`.

2. `mv` (Move): Move or rename files or directories with `mv`. To rename 'file1.txt' to 'file3.txt', type `mv file1.txt file3.txt`.

3. `rm` (Remove): Delete files with `rm`. For instance, to delete 'file1.txt', type `rm file1.txt`.

4. `mkdir` (Make Directory): This command helps you create a new directory. To create a directory named 'newdir', type `mkdir newdir`.

5. `rmdir` (Remove Directory): This command allows you to delete a directory. Keep in mind, the directory should be empty. To delete a directory named 'newdir', type `rmdir newdir`.

5.4. Raspberry Pi Networking Commands

1. `ifconfig` : It details the current network status of your Pi. Use it to get your IP address details and other networking parameters.

2. `iwconfig` : This command gives you information about your wireless network status.

3. `ping`: Determine the status of your network connectivity with this command. For instance, to check if Google is reachable, type `ping www.google.com`.

5.5. Raspberry Pi Configuration Commands

1. `raspi-config` : This command calls the Raspberry Pi Software Configuration Tool, which allows you to adjust various settings on your Pi like the password, display options, etc.

2. `gpio readall` : This command provides detailed information about the status of GPIO pins, which is particularly beneficial in electronics projects.

Remember, the Linux command line is forgiving to a degree. Use the `Tab` button for autocomplete, and feel free to explore and learn. Be careful with commands like 'rm', as they can swiftly erase files and directories. Always double-check what you're typing before you hit Enter.

5.6. Installing and Updating Software on Raspberry Pi

Aptitude (apt) is an interface to the Debian GNU/Linux package system. It allows you to seamlessly manage your Raspberry Pi's software packages.

1. `sudo apt-get update` : This command updates the list of available packages and their version, but it does not install or upgrade any packages.

2. `sudo apt-get upgrade` : After updating the package list with the above command, use this command to upgrade all the installed packages on your Pi.

3. `sudo apt-get install <package_name>` : This command allows you to install a software package. Replace <package_name> with the name of the software package you want to install.

That's your primer on the essential Raspberry Pi commands. While it might feel overwhelming initially, familiarize yourself with these basic commands. Be patient, and in time, you'll be able to navigate through the Linux environment more efficiently and run your Raspberry Pi effortlessly.

Chapter 6. DIY Project 1: Building a Retro Gaming Console

Starting on the journey of creating your very own retro gaming console using the Raspberry Pi is a fascinating and fulfilling venture. There's something magical about playing games from days of yore on a console you've built yourself. The process might seem daunting at first, but fear not. We'll take you step by step, breaking down the complexities to make it as straightforward as possible.

6.1. Gather Your Materials

First things first. Before we can start assembling and coding, we need to gather the necessary materials.

Here's the essential list:

- Raspberry Pi 3 or above

- MicroSD card (minimum 16 GB)

- MicroSD card reader

- USB keyboard and mouse

- HDMI cable

- Monitor or TV with HDMI input

- Power supply (5V/2.5A for Raspberry Pi 3 and 5V/3A for Raspberry Pi 4)

- RetroPie software

For the housing or casing of the console, you have multiple options:

- Purchase a prefabricated Raspberry Pi case

- 3D print a custom case

- Build your own using everyday materials

6.2. Preparing the Raspberry Pi

Once you have everything ready, it's time to prepare the Raspberry Pi. This includes installing the operating system and configuring it for the first time.

Download the RetroPie software, which will serve as our gaming operating system, from the official RetroPie website. Choose the correct version depending upon your Raspberry Pi model. Once the file is downloaded, you'll get a .gz file, which you have to extract to get the .img file.

Next, we will use software like "Win32 Disk Imager" or "Etcher" to copy this RetroPie image on our MicroSD card. To do this, insert the memory card into your computer using the reader and open up the imaging software. Select the .img file you just extracted, choose your MicroSD card from the options list, and click on "Write". This process can take some time and will format your MicroSD card, so ensure any necessary data has been backed up.

Finally, remove the MicroSD card from the reader and insert it into the Raspberry Pi.

6.3. Building the Console

Plug in your HDMI cable to the Raspberry Pi and your TV or monitor. Connect the USB keyboard and mouse. Finally, plug in the power supply to power up the Raspberry Pi. The Raspberry Pi should boot up, and you should see the RetroPie Splash on your screen after which the Welcome configuration screen will appear, indicating a successful setup.

Once the startup has finished, you will need to configure your controls. For most users, it will be setting up the controller you'll use for playing games.

6.4. Configuring the Controller

Configuring game controllers on RetroPie is simple. Plug in your controller, RetroPie will detect it. Hold down any button on your controller until the configuration screen appears. Assign functions to the corresponding buttons on your controller by pressing them when prompted. If there are more buttons than your controller has, just hold down any button to bypass these steps. Once you're finished, select the "OK" option.

6.5. Adding the Games

The legalities around ROMs (game files) are a bit murky. It's generally acceptable to possess ROM games if you own the original. Essentially, it counts as having a digital backup.

Assuming you have obtained your ROMs, the next step is to put them on your Raspberry Pi. The easiest way to do this is through a USB stick. Create a folder named "retropie" in your USB stick. Plug this USB stick into the Pi and wait for it to stop blinking. This will create directories inside the "retropie" folder for each console system supported.

Remove the USB stick, plug it back into your computer, and copy your ROMs onto the correct system's directory. For example, NES games go in the "nes" folder.

Once done, plug the USB stick back into the Raspberry Pi. The Pi will automatically transfer the ROMs from the USB to the microSD card.

6.6. Final Test Run

After the transfer finishes, navigate back to the RetroPie home menu. Here, you will start seeing different console options, each containing the corresponding games you added. Pick any game and start playing.

Let's wrap up this chapter. You have just built a cool Raspberry Pi console that plays classic games! This project is a fun way to dive into the world of Raspberry Pi–it combines building, programming, and a dash of nostalgia.

Stay tuned and keep exploring. Our next project promises to be as exciting and inspiring as this one!

Chapter 7. DIY Project 2: Setting Up a Home Automation System

Let's jump in, by setting the stage to automate your home using Raspberry Pi. The goal underlining this project is to transform your household into a smart home model, taking control of many singular, everyday tasks. These tasks may include the likes of controlling room temperature, lighting, door locks, windows, music, and much more using simple Python programming language.

7.1. Understanding Home Automation

Home automation, or domotics, refers to the automatic control of household features, activities, and appliances. Various control systems are utilized in this residential extension of building automation. This technology implements electrical devices in the house to be remotely controlled from any internet-connected place in the world by employing a mobile or other networked device. A home automation system will control lighting, climate, entertainment systems, appliances, and home security such as access control and alarm systems.

When connected with the Internet, home devices form an integral part of the 'Internet of Things' (IoT). A home automation system typically connects to various home appliances to a central hub or "gateway". The user interface for control of the system employs either wall-mounted terminals, mobile phone software, or web-based interfaces, often but not always via Internet cloud services.

7.2. Pre-requisites

Before embarking on the journey to automate your home, it's imperative to gather all the necessary elements that'll be pivotal in the process. Below is a list of the pre-requisites:

- Raspberry Pi board (Preferably Raspberry Pi 3 or newer)

- SD Card (8 GB and Above)

- Wi-Fi Dongle (If the board doesn't have built-in Wi-Fi)

- Power Supply

- Breadboard, Jumper wires & Resistors

- Various sensors and devices like motion detectors, temperature sensors, humidity sensors, door sensors, light sensors, and cameras.

- Relay

- Python installed on Raspberry Pi to develop home automation system

7.3. Installation of Home Assistant Software

One of the most important parts of setting up a home automation system using Raspberry Pi is the installation of home automation software. There are several different home automation platforms out there, and Home Assistant is one of the most popular among them. The installation procedure will vary depending on the software you choose, but here, we will be using Home Assistant.

DIY Project 3: Creating a Portable Computer

One of the great things about Raspberry Pi is its versatility. There's this popular project among tech enthusiasts: creating a portable computer. Let's get started on this exciting journey, showing you each step of the process in detail.

Gathering Your Materials

Before we dive in, we need to gather all the necessities.

1. Raspberry Pi 3 Model B or B+

2. 7" Touchscreen Display for Raspberry Pi

3. MicroSD Card (recommend 32GB Sandisk Extreme Pro)

4. Wireless Keyboard and Mouse

5. Power Supply (5V/2.5A) for Raspberry Pi

6. Portable 10000mAh Battery Pack

7. Case for Raspberry Pi and 7" Touchscreen Display

8. Micro USB cable

Configuring Your Raspberry Pi

To get started, you'll need to have Raspbian, the Raspberry Pi's official supported OS, installed on your microSD Card. You can download the latest version of Raspbian from the Raspberry Pi website. Once you've downloaded the .img file, you can use an image burning tool like Etcher to install it on your microSD card. Insert the card in your Raspberry Pi.

Setting up the Screen

Your next key task is setting up the display. Connect your 7" touchscreen display to the Raspberry Pi with the ribbon cable that comes with the screen. The connection port is right on the side of the Pi. Power on the Raspberry Pi and you should see the boot-up sequence on the display.

Getting Raspberry Pi Online

Connect a mouse and a keyboard to your Raspberry Pi. You'll need them to navigate the interface initially. Connect your Raspberry Pi to your local Wi-Fi network by clicking on the network icon on the top-right corner of your screen.

Updating the System

Once connected to the internet, open the terminal window (should be on the top bar) and type in the following commands to update your Pi:

```
sudo apt-get update
sudo apt-get upgrade -y
```

These commands ensure that your Raspberry Pi has the latest firmware and software patches.

Installing LibreOffice

Your portable computer wouldn't be complete without the capabilities to produce documents, make spreadsheets, or create presentations. You can install LibreOffice, a free powerful office suite, with the following command in terminal:

```
sudo apt-get install libreoffice -y
```

Setting up Pi Power Management

In order to use the Pi as a portable computer, you have to set proper power management. You need to tweak various power management settings with the help of 'TLP', which is an advanced power management tool for Linux:

```
sudo apt-get install tlp tlp-rdw -y
sudo systemctl enable tlp
```

Packing it All Up

Now, place your Raspberry Pi and the touchscreen into the case. Make sure you have easy access to the power port of your Pi. Connect the Pi to the power bank via the micro USB cable.

Congratulations! You've just crafted a portable Raspberry Pi computer. With this power in your hands, you can take it anywhere, from work to cafes, libraries, meetings, or on road trips. From here, the possibilities are endless. You can further customize this gadget to add more functions according to your needs. Remember, the fun of this involves not just the result, but also the journey of tinkering and enhancing your project along the way. With patience and creativity, you can transform this tiny board into a reliable companion that serves your individual computing needs perfectly.

Chapter 8. In-depth Analysis: Troubleshooting Common Raspberry Pi Issues

Let's begin by exploring common issues related to Raspberry Pi: power and bootup issues, software problems, and hardware-related complications. Moreover, we will be delving into various methods for debugging and resolving these problems.

8.1. Understanding Power Problems

A very common issue Raspberry Pi users face relate to insufficient power. The Raspberry Pi, especially the later models (3 and 4), require a substantial amount of power to operate efficiently. A power rating of between 2.5A to 3A is advisable. Lesser current could lead to unexpected behavior or, in some instances, not powering on at all.

.Identifying Power Issues

Whenever the lightning bolt symbol or a low voltage warning appears on your screen, it indicates that your Raspberry Pi isn't receiving enough power. This can lead to reduced performance or even data corruption.

.Troubleshooting Power Issues

There are different approaches to resolving power issues. Firstly, ensure you're using a power supply specifically recommended for your Raspberry Pi model. A smartphone charger might not suffice. You can also use a powered USB hub to ensure adequate power supply.

8.2. Working With Bootup Issues

Another common issue makers face with Raspberry Pi is the device failing to boot. This problem usually arises because of SD card issues or incorrectly installed OS.

.Identifying Bootup Issues

One way you can tell if your Raspberry Pi has booting issues is when the red LED light is on, but the green LED light either flickers inconsistently or doesn't light up at all.

.Troubleshooting Booting Issues

Ensure that your SD card is working correctly. Test it in another device, and if it's not working there as well, you might need to replace it. If the SD card works fine, the problem could be the OS. Download the latest version and install it onto the SD card.

8.3. Conquering Software Problems

Just like any other computer, the Raspberry Pi doesn't escape software issues. These can range from a non-responsive system, to failed installations, to issues while programming.

.Identifying Software Problems

Not being able to perform functions that worked perfectly before, receiving multiple error messages, or even finding your Raspberry Pi unresponsive, all these are clear indications of software trouble.

.Troubleshooting Software Problems

Resolving software issues primarily involves troubleshooting the OS or the program causing the problem. Update your Pi and also the problematic software to the most recent version. If the issues persist, consider creating a backup of important files and installing the OS again.

=== Hardware Complications

Sometimes, you may encounter issues with Raspberry Pi peripherals like the camera, GPIO pins, or even multiple devices connected via USB.

_.Identifying Hardware Problems _

When a peripheral that was working fine earlier suddenly stops functioning, it's a clear sign of hardware trouble. Moreover, a dedicated error message is displayed when a utility like the Raspberry Pi camera fails.

.Troubleshooting Hardware Issues

The first step is to gently unplug, check, and then replug the device. If it still malfunctions, test the peripheral with an alternative Raspberry Pi if possible. Check if the hardware is compatible with your Raspberry Pi model. For GPIO problems, a multimeter can help debug the issue.

8.4. Optimizing Troubleshooting Methods

It's essential to remain systematic while debugging issues on your Raspberry Pi. Following a methodical approach ensures you inspect every aspect from hardware to software, ensuring no stone is left unturned in the quest to extract optimum performance from your Pi.

.Keep System Up To Date

Ensure your OS, libraries, and software are updated regularly. This eliminates potential bugs that can hamper performance.

.Use Diagnostic Tools

If you're dealing with complex issues, software like 'Raspberry Pi Diagnostic Tool' can be helpful to check the actual problem.

.Consult Raspberry Pi Communities

If you're encountering a new problem, it's likely that someone else has already faced it and found a solution. Raspberry Pi forums are an excellent resource for finding solutions.

In summary, troubleshooting Raspberry Pi issues involves applying a process of elimination to identify the problem and then following proven steps to solve it. Whether you're dealing with power issues, bootup problems, software glitches, or hardware failures, knowing what to look for and how to fix it can ensure your Raspberry Pi provides the performance, reliability, and enjoyment you expect.

Chapter 9. Advanced Techniques: Enhancing Your Raspberry Pi Skills

Mastering the Raspberry Pi is not just about getting familiar with its basic functionalities. It's equally about pushing the boundaries, testing the waters of innovation, and acquiring advanced skills to leverage this credit card-sized wonder tool to its maximum potential.

9.1. Pin Configuration and GPIO Understanding

Raspberry Pi comes along with a set of 40 pins that are located on the edge of the board, often referred to as the GPIO (General Purpose Input Output) pins. Understanding the GPIO pins opens the door to a vast variety of projects that could be carried out using Raspberry Pi. Here's a basic rundown.

NOTE	Exercise caution while dealing with the GPIO Pins. Incorrect use can lead to permanent damage.

We'll first go through the pin configuration of Raspberry Pi. It has numbered two ways - physical pins (the actual number of the pin) and GPIO pins (the BCM number of the pin).

9.1.1. Physical Pins

This is the basic numbering of Raspberry Pi's 40 pins and it starts from top left and ends at bottom right.

```
1 - 3V3           2 - 5V
```

```
3 - GPIO02        4 - 5V
5 - GPIO03        6 - GND
7 - GPIO04        8 - GPIO14
9 - GND          10 - GPIO15

.
.
.
39 - GND         40 - GPIO21
```

 3V3 indicates 3.3 volts, 5V indicates 5 volts, and GND represents Ground.

9.1.2. GPIO Pins

This is the Broadcom numbering, or BCM numbering for short, and represents the number given by Raspberry Pi's makers.

```
1 - 3V3           2 - 5V
3 - GPIO2         4 - 5V
5 - GPIO3         6 - GND
7 - GPIO4         8 - GPIO14
9 - GND          10 - GPIO15

.
.
.
39 - GND         40 - GPIO21
```

Remember, the GPIO numbering is different from the physical pin configuration.

9.2. Interfacing with Hardware

The true versatility of Raspberry Pi comes alive when you start interfacing it with hardware components. This essentially means connecting additional components such as LEDs, switches, sensors, etc., to the Pi to create more sophisticated projects.

9.2.1. Interfacing Raspberry Pi with LED

To get a taste of hardware interfacing, we'll start with an elementary project – lighting up an LED.

IMPORTANT A resistor is necessary for this experiment to prevent damage to the LED.

Gather the following components: * Breadboard * Jumper wires * LED * 220-ohm Resistor

The following steps walk you through a simple GPIO project:

1. Identify the anode (longer lead) and the cathode (shorter lead) of the LED.

2. Insert the anode into the GPIO18 pin and cathode into any of the ground pins.

3. Bind the GPIO18 pin to output using the 'gpio -g mode 18 out' command.

4. To turn on the LED, use 'gpio -g write 18 1'.

5. To turn it off, use 'gpio -g write 18 0'.

--- continue to explain other hardware interfacing such as with sensors, motors etc.

9.3. Navigating around Linux

If you're using Raspberry Pi OS for your projects, you'll essentially be interacting with a version of Linux. Thus, mastering certain Linux skills can enhance your Raspberry Pi experience.

--- continue to go in detail explaining Linux commands, permissions, scripts etc.

9.4. Networking and Raspberry Pi

Raspberry Pi also allows networking operations for IoT projects, where the devices need to communicate with each other.

--- continue to detail out networking principles, protocols and how Raspberry Pi can make use of them.

9.5. Advanced Python Programming for Raspberry Pi

Python is a versatile language that offers vast library support and efficient framing of logic and can be used in conjunction with Raspberry Pi to create amazing projects.

--- continue with more advanced Python programming tutorials specifically beneficial for Raspberry Pi.

This chapter may seem daunting at first due to its in-depth insight into multiple aspects. However, each topic is paramount for your journey of Mastering Raspberry Pi. We suggest working through each sub-chapter, testing and re-testing every experiment until attained success. Patience is key, experts weren't built in a day. Happy experimenting!

NOTE Always ensure precautions while handling the physical aspects of the Raspberry Pi or any other electronic components involved to avoid any chances of damage to the devices or person involved.

Keep in mind that the Raspberry Pi is not just a gadget but a tool for imagination, a way to explore the world of electronics and computing and to make your ideas take a physical and tangible form! So, let's keep exploring and keep learning.

Chapter 10. Next Steps: Broadening Your Raspberry Pi Project Horizons

You've spent time understanding the basics and maybe even created your first Raspberry Pi (R-Pi) project. That is a huge milestone. Still, you might wonder, "What's next? How do I expand my Raspberry Pi horizons?" In this vital section of the report, we examine ways to push your Pi skills further, exploring more complex and enriching projects, getting involved in the Raspberry Pi community, and turning your innovative ideas into reality.

10.1. Advancement through Projects

The Raspberry Pi's flexibility enables you to take on a wide array of projects. Here are a handful of advanced concepts to get your gears turning:

10.1.1. Home Automation Projects

Home automation can be a useful and interesting way to create an efficient and smart living environment. In essence, it means using devices and sensors to monitor and control your household appliances and systems. Some automation projects ideas you can consider are:

```
* Smart Thermostat: This can be programmed to compute
the most efficient way to heat your home and can be
controlled remotely.
* Automated Lighting: Having set your preferences, the
lighting gets adjusted depending on time of day or
occupancy.
```

* Security Systems: Create a Raspberry Pi powered
security system that sends alerts to your phone when
something triggers it.

Learning how to integrate different sensors and devices will provide
valuable experience as well.

10.1.2. Retro Gaming Stations

Creating a gaming station using Raspberry Pi is also an exciting
venture, providing nostalgia and fun. Whether locally or over a
network, Raspberry Pi can emulate various old school arcade and
console games. You gain knowledge on emulation and using
Raspberry Pi with other devices like gamepad controllers.

10.1.3. Internet of Things (IoT) Devices

Internet of Things involves interconnecting multiple devices over the
internet and has been prolifically climbing in popularity. Some
interesting projects to consider:

* Weather Station: A Raspberry Pi weather station can
gauge temperature, humidity, pressure, and even air
quality.
* Health Monitor: A Raspberry Pi can be combined with
various sensors to create a compact health monitor
system for heart rate, blood pressure, etc.

IoT projects help you tap into concepts like data governance, cyber
security, and networking.

10.1.4. Programming Robots

Building a robot might feel like a massive leap, but it's an adventurous path to self-discover and learn about coding, mechanics, and electronics.

10.2. Developing Your Skills

More challenging projects might require knowledge outside of the Raspberry Pi. Undertaking these projects allows you to understand new programming languages, hardware systems, and networking concepts.

10.2.1. Learning Advanced Programming

Depending on the project, you might need to expand your conventionally used programming languages list. Languages like C++, JAVA, or Python libraries like NumPy for number crunching can aid your Raspberry Pi journey.

10.2.2. Exploring Electronics

Learning about Circuit Design, PCBs (Printed Circuit Boards), soldering techniques, and using oscilloscopes could be the next destination for your Raspberry Pi journey.

10.3. Expanding Your Horizon

However, projects and learning new skills are just a part of expanding your Pi horizons.

10.3.1. Joining a Raspberry Pi Community

Joining a Raspberry Pi community will offer numerous benefits. You can learn from more experienced users, help novices, share your experiences, and keep up with the latest advancements. A few notable ones include the official Raspberry Pi forum, GitHub, and StackExchange.

10.3.2. Starting a Raspberry Pi Club

Starting a Raspberry Pi club at school or in your local community can also be a great way to share your enthusiasm for Raspberry Pi and foster a supportive learning atmosphere for all.

10.4. Transforming Your Ideas into Implementation

At this point, you might have many grand concepts you wish to implement. Planning and following through is key. Managing a larger project requires prioritization, proper documentation, and testing. Collaboration tools like GitHub, Trello, or Jira can help manage and track your project's process.

10.5. Conclusion

Broadening your Raspberry Pi horizon is a step by step learning process but, more importantly, it's an exciting journey of discovery and innovation. Stay patient, be relentless, and let your curiosity continue to evolve your projects. Most importantly, enjoy each project for the unique learning journey it offers, and remember, every Raspberry Pi Master was once a novice who decided not to give up.

With these advanced projects and ideas, your mastery of Raspberry Pi is bound to reach new levels. Happy tinkering! Don't forget to share your amazing innovations with the world.